Even Before
My Own
Name

Also by Tracy Koretsky

NOVEL
Ropeless

BOOK INCLUSIONS
"Learning the Language" (story) in *Where We Find Ourselves: Jewish Women around the World Write about Home*; edited by Miriam Ben-Yoseph and Deborah Nodler Rosen (SUNY: 2009).

"*La Poire Hautaine*" (essay) in *Poem, Revised: 54 Poems, Discussions, Revisions*; edited by Robert Hartwell Fiske and Laura Cherry (Marion Street Press: 2008).

For audio poems, author interviews, and links to short fiction, essays, reviews, and more poems, visit: www.TracyKoretsky.com.

Even Before My Own Name

poems by
Tracy Koretsky

ragged bottom
press

Copyright © 2009 by Tracy Koretsky
Printed in the United States of America

All rights reserved. No part of this book may be reproduced in any manner without written consent except for the quotation of short passages used in an article, critique, or review.

ragged bottom press
Berkeley, CA

cover design and photography: Sherry Bloom

ISBN: 0-9841242-0-9

Acknowledgements

Grateful acknowledgement is made to the following publications in which some of these poems have appeared, sometimes in earlier forms:

The Alembic: "The Moment She Discovered She Was Mortal"
Binnacle: "Community Property"
California Quarterly: "*Yahrzeit*"
Coal City Review: "I guess he's dead now,"
Cold Mountain: "The Stories of Survivors"
Comstock Review: "beginning"
Curbside Review: "Blond and Strawberry-skinned"
The Eleventh Muse: "*Yahrzeit*"
The First Decade Anthology: "The Night that Megan Called"
Fourth River: "A Letter from Academe"
Fresh Ground: "On an Asphalt Playground, 1972"
Georgetown Review: "A Poem for Leaving Pittsburgh"
Habersham Review: "Blond and Strawberry-skinned"
Haiku Harvest: "the sound of waves"
Home Planet News: "On an Asphalt Playground, 1972"
Israel Horizons: "The Stories of Survivors"
Jabberwock Review: "Community Property"
The Kerf: "The Wisdom of Stones"
Lilliput: "Dear Rejection,"
Mark: "The Night that Megan Called"
North Central Review: "On an Asphalt Playground, 1972"
Offerings: "Is This Not the Nature of Obsession?"
On the Outskirts (Inglis House): "Blond and Strawberry-skinned"
Out of Line: Poems of Social Justice (Garden House Press): "*Pietà*"
Oyez: "The Moment She Discovered She Was Mortal"
The Panhandler: "The Wisdom of Stones"
Phantasmagoria: "Mismatched Baggage"
Pittsburgh and Tri-State Area Poets Anthology: "Vespers"
Pittsburgh Post Gazette: "The Wisdom of Stones"
The Pittsburgh Quarterly: "The Day I Suffered from Temporary Incapability"
Poetica: "Learning to Be Good at the Jewish Home for the Aged"
Poetry Motel: "For Emily, on the Staten Island Ferry" and "Vespers"
Potomac Review: "*Yahrzeit*"
Response: "The Stories of Survivors"
Riverrun: "The Day I Suffered from Temporary Incapability" and "Vespers"
Simply Haiku: "Brief Thaw"
Sketchbook: "and tomorrow, green again"
stet: "I guess he's dead now," and "A Poem for No One's Dog"
The Sucharnochee Review: "À la Place de la Bastille, La Fête de la Musique"

Sulphur River Literary Review: "The Stories of Survivors"
Triplopia: "Community Property" and "fade to white"
Uncapped: "À la Place de la Bastille, La Fête de la Musique"
White Pelican: "Vespers"
Wordgathering: "Blond and Strawberry-skinned"

The poems in this collection have also received the following recognitions:

"Community Property" and "On an Asphalt Playground, 1972" have been nominated for Pushcart Prizes.

"Community Property" also received First Prize from Gotham Writers.

"The Wisdom of Stones" received First Prize from *Wanton Words*, an Honorable Mention from *Shadow Poetry*, and an Honorable Mention from *Nashville Newsletter*.

"*Pietà*" received First Prize in the Oneswan Writing Competition.

"Melting into Water" received Second Prize from *The Blind Man's Rainbow*.

"*Yahrzeit*" received Second Prize from NPAC and an Honorable Mention from the Alabama Writers' Association.

"For Emily, on the Staten Island Ferry" was a finalist in NPAC and received an Honorable Mention from the Arizona Authors' Association.

"The Moment She Discovered She was Mortal" was a finalist in NPAC.

"beginning" received an Honorable Mention from *Shadow Poetry*.

"fade to white" received an Honorable Mention from the League of PEN Women.

"Mismatched Baggage" received an Honorable Mention from the Kentucky State Poetry Society.

"Solitaire" received an Honorable Mention from *The Blind Man's Rainbow*.

"the sound of rain" received an Honorable Mention from the Washington Poets' Association.

"When the Call Comes: Notes Towards Revision" was performed with an original score by Eliza Shefler at the Berkeley Art Center, March, 2008.

The author would like to thank the Squirrel Hill Poets of Pittsburgh, Pennsylvania, without whom this collection could not have been possible. Special thanks to Naomi Ruth Lowinsky, Tobey Kaplan, and Jendi Reiter for their patience and insights.

to the girl I once was

Contents

I

- 13 The Wisdom of Stones
- 14 Once, in Soho,
- 15 Solitaire
- 18 Hidden Behind the Middle School
- 20 Melting into Water
- 21 *Pietà*
- 23 *Yahrzeit*

II

- 27 You Were a Son of a Bitch to Me My Whole Life and I Can't Really Think of One Nice Thing You Ever Did For Me, Except This:
- 28 The Moment She Discovered She Was Mortal
- 29 Mismatched Baggage
- 31 Learning to Be Good at the Jewish Home for the Elderly
- 33 On an Asphalt Playground, 1972
- 35 The Corner
- 37 Unwrapped
- 39 A Brief Thaw
- 40 A Poem for No One's Dog
- 42 I guess he's dead now,
- 43 In the Half-Light Before the JCC Single Parents' Event, 1978
- 45 Community Property
- 46 The Stories of Survivors

III

51 The Day I Suffered from Temporary Incapability
52 and tomorrow, green again
53 Is This Not the Nature of Obsession?
55 wave
56 Dear Rejection,
58 For Emily, On The Staten Island Ferry
60 The Night that Megan Called
61 Blond and Strawberry-skinned
63 A Letter from Academe
65 A Poem for Leaving Pittsburgh
66 fade to white
69 until...

IV

73 When The Call Comes: Notes Towards Revision
83 Conclusion

V

87   beginning
88   Dead or Alive: My Mothers Side, 1985
95   Cousins, Unbraided
98   With This Book
99   Wanting Land
101 *À La Place De La Bastille, La Fête De La Musique*
103 Naked at 45
105 Vespers

I

The Wisdom of Stones

Treat trouble like
a smooth gray stone
Turn it over in your
hand; its weight is
solid. Press it cool
against your cheek;
it does not yield. Then
cast it far into the
waters. Watch it echo

…then forget

Once, in Soho,

I descended into damp, whitewashed cavern, brushed beside
her ruby curtain, and gave my hand. Her gravel voice lisped light
through brown   broken   teeth sounding of cypress
recesses along the Mediterranean coast, and her hair, silver
with lamplight, lifted like dandelion in seed. She stroked

and traced my heart line back, almost to
my knuckles, found my knowledge
line, flattered it was long and deep. "So,"
she soothed, "You have been to school,
but still, you have not learned how we breathe."

Then she made of me
a fist—heart against knowledge—and together
we took into us

all the air in the room
as if   about   to sing, or   perhaps,

to float.

Solitaire

Daddy, you are an orange arc of ember
glowing belly to lip
        belly to lip
on your side of the bed
beside the pornography drawer
next to the glass—
Kentucky bourbon—poured
        repoured.
Except for your drag on your cigarette,
        your occasional cough,
all sleeps
beneath the cover of your mood.

You have been there two days this time.

        Later, awake,
        woozy and walking, eyes
        shaded like a man emerging
        from a tunnel, you settle
        yourself before Mom's Danish pine
        in your Chicago suburban home.
        You blink and you remember: You live here.
        You own this home,
                this table, those chairs.
        Everything you see is yours
        everything you touch
        as long as the bank is paid

            —You did pay the bank—

Yes, you think you paid the bank.

    You reach
           shuffle.
Slippery, square,
—like all those so-called friends.
They lay flat, neat beside the next.
Seven hopeful times,
so this time,
      one time,
      tonight,
you may win.

              See? Red five covers black six.
              Imagine the opportunity!
              King starts a new dynasty!
              Ace a new order!
              Turn and show,
                  stack
                  and snap.
              Then, finger your reserve
              one,
                    whisper, "Come on"
              two,
                    "Come on this time
                three,
                  flip and…
                  fickle they forsake you.
Reshuffle,
      reshuffle,
the night is long and always the same.

***

      Morning: a suggestion soon insisting.
      You empty the ashtray, fill the ready glass,
      eyes to carpet, find the stairs, the bed,
           the stairs, the bed,
           the dark, the day.

Daddy, you are an orange arc of ember
glowing belly to lip   belly to lip
beside me in the next room
as I dress for school.
In the threshold of morning
I press your door with my open palm
It gives. It is not locked.
I whisper, "Did you win?"
"No," you say, "but I didn't cheat."
"Maybe tonight," I sigh, already late and turning.
Too late already, and turned.

Hidden Behind the Middle School
> *for Mark*

I remember my brother as a Puerto Rican
in the loose dust gravel backways of Chicago
after his fight with Dad when
fists slid to slam.

In the loose dust gravel backways of Chicago
he wandered, still figuring how
fists slid to slam and
and the street became home.

He wandered, still figuring how
he would make it now,
and the street became home.
He told me, hidden behind the middle school,

he would make out now.
He always was smart.
He told me, hidden behind the middle school,
"I can sell my pretty ass,"

—he always was smart—
"or I can sell drugs.
I can sell my pretty ass."
Then he wriggled, proving it.

"Or I can sell drugs.
I already like drugs."
Then he wriggled, proving it.
I wanted my brother to come home.

"I already like drugs
too," I told him.
I wanted my brother to come home.
"You always were clever," he said.

"Too," I told him.
And then I said,
"You always were—"   "Clever?" he said.
"No. A gringo."

And then I said,
"What gives?"
"No, a 'gringo,'
that's not my problem.

What gives
is you don't wanna be a skinny Jew-kid out there, but
that's not my problem.
—not anymore," he said.

"You don't wanna be a skinny Jew-kid out there? But
you can still be yourself with me."
"Not anymore," he said,
one fully fall afternoon.

"You can still be yourself with me,"
I cried, stamping my foot like the girl I was
one fully fall afternoon
watching my brother leave me.

I cried, stamping my foot like the girl I was
still for many years to come, and
watching my brother leave me
became just another event.

Still, for many years to come, and
after my fight with Dad
became just another event,
I remember my brother as a Puerto Rican.

Melting into Water

Stone Mother buried beneath the ground
beneath the growing daughter.
Wind Father laid himself down, down,

unwinged, floating, sans a sound,
melting into water.
Stone Mother buried beneath the ground

unable to feed one still so unfound
so much still not taught her.
Wind Father laid himself down, down,

down, lay wounded, open, his bile unbound,
ahowl like a pig to the slaughter.
Stone Mother buried beneath the ground

had she a face, would wear a frown
to see how his cries had caught her.
Wind Father laid himself down, down;

the canyons wailed with his echo's resound
wind-whipping the waves of his daughter.
Stone Mother buried beneath the ground.
Wind Father laid himself down, down.

Pietà

Just before the end we watched you there, stretched out
across your mama's lap, her strong young man, silent, cold;

your eyes closed. I leaned toward the screen when they showed
Mary's face, all the sorrow in the world in them stone eyes.

Newslady said some sad soul splattered red paint across
your chest, across your mama's face. I wondered if

it made a tear. Said the madman tried to break you apart
with a hammer. Couldn't do it though. Takes more than that,

I know. Don't have to say nothing; a mother just knows.
So I told him he might as well fall in love with a rich man

as a poor one. I told him, "You be careful," you know.
He promised he was. Got scared when I caught him

rubbing his throat. I made him see that doctor myself.
That doctor. Had to wear a mask and robe just to see my son,

had to use gloves to touch his hair, straight and thin like a white
boy's. He hated to see me coming at him like that; he'd say, "Let me

see your face, Mama." "No, son." I had to say. Nearly broke
us both in two. So I took him home. Hospital's no place for a boy

to die. Quit my job, brought him cookies. He'd eat bag after bag;
always offer me some. I wasn't sure, but I ate anyway. Then

my boy would groan and curl. I knew what I had to do. Roll him
over, untape the padding, soak the rag in the bucket, wring it,

wring it, pat on the powder with my gloved hand, saying "Never
you mind, son."   My son.

If your Mama didn't shed no tears it was 'cause she never had to
powder your thirty-year-old bottom. Oh, I know you got your

reasons, ain't for me to question in this life, but as a mother,
you know, I gotta say: You wanted my boy, Lord? Then

you hold him near. You let his pretty voice rise up in your choir.
You greedy for my boy, Lord? So bad you couldn't wait

just thirty years? Then tell your mama to touch his hair without
gloves, Lord, without masks. I never got to hold my baby

cool across my lap. Mortician made me pay extra just to clean
him. Now, before you go and listen to someone else's troubles

I want to say I saw that statue again: on a card at the Well-Mart.
Opened it real fast. It said nothing, just…nothing. I took it home.

Put it in his drawer, under the paper. Put a lock
on the door so I can sleep nights. Sometimes I wonder

if they got the thing cleaned off. I dream of rags in buckets
of red, Mary's stone hand wringing   wringing.

Yahrzeit
    (the anniversary of a death)

You are just stone, Mama
in my life longer dead than alive
you sink   gray   bloodless
away from me faster each year
I plunge the waters
fish the few facts
five foot one   clear blue eyes   thirty-nine
You sang mornings as I do now
loved your kitchen
the tangerine and lemon placemats
—ugly colors that ruin my appetite—
and you laughed, I think, surely you must have
but you took that too, more dead mama
took all the money for your Chemo
took the cousins and the thanksgivings
and left me a stone
I've never visited
but for the time it was laid
a pale young girl in a skirt no one noticed she'd outgrown
the color of granite darkened by dew
whose lips moved without prayer
for you'd taken the religion
and left me
with this baby name I have for you
holding a mop and bucket to clean up everyone's tears
and the smudges of your fingers from the bedroom wall
pack Dad bologna on white bread
sew both brothers' buttons
fear the weight of my breasts
spot my panties
You left me
to stand before the choir alone singing into darkness
and because you were not there to see me walk across the stage
I did not walk across the stage
Because you will not join me beneath the canopy

I will have no canopy
And children?
Oh, Mama, I could never leave children
standing in a field of broken stones
So I lay aside this sculptor's chisel
I use you now
to step across the river
If I bow to face the waters
it is I that am reflected
my voice that rises above the morning
It is I who bleed   all by myself
every one of my living months
Aw, you can keep your death, Mama
'cause your baby girl
has got pockets full of stones
and a slingshot, Mama
and a slingshot

II

You Were a Son of a Bitch to Me My Whole Life and I Can't Really Think of One Nice Thing You Ever Did For Me, Except This:

whirling
around
the cul-de-sac,
around
the little tree
growing
in the cement ring
in the clean new dirt
of the cul-de-sac,
my little rear up
off the banana seat,
legs pumping,
my sissy bar
leaning,
I flew
and tore
my leg
bright
open, and,
as if from the sky,
like some guy
too much in a hurry
to grab his cape, you
swooped down,
sweeping me
into your arms,
shouting
for Mom.

The Moment She Discovered She Was Mortal

Mama's marriage hand
clutched the wild wheel
releasing our tires
to the ice.
Her right arm steeled like a gate
across my body. Her mouth
w i d e w a i l s i r e n e d   One
sheer cliff of sound
Trees spun away
      then buildings
           then trees buildings
                  treesbuildings
   And when we stopped
our tires were already
in the woods.

Mama swallowed
her arm, a stiff half-crucifix,
      then felt me
          turned me
               front to back
      tenfingers
     tentoes
cooed, "My baby, my baby"
though I was a girl of eight.
She nodded
let
her head fall,
then coughpuddlesobbed
an unclear rain
on the still winter wheel.

Mismatched Baggage

Nineteen and certainlynot married
I boarded "Mrs." to Michael
because, in 1979, marrieds
saved forty, soon spent
on figs rolled in a powder of nuts
just four, wrapped
in four different colors of cellophane,
and soy shakes in boxes, several each,
with straws made from pasta
because it biodegrades.
I'd made sandwiches, spread
almond butter and honey between
uneven, handcut whole grain,
wrapped them in wax paper
like origami gifts.   Tried.

But a wife? She would have known Michael's allergies.
Known to nag.   So much gin
proposed and toasted
at each unwrapped helping
as helpful as hives.
Sullen, he brushed his blues,
his guitar and long legs stretching the aisle.
He'd done his job.   Had he?
And what then did we imagine a certainlynothusband for?
To handle, perhaps, the few willing bags?
To open his case in the station
and strum for tossed quarters and the smiles of passing-by girls?
He'd brought the gin,
the traveling jigger, two bottles of tonic, three whole fresh limes.
Well done then, for he'd brought peace,
guised though as stupor, jolting above shuddersqueal
brakes, blurring the lines on the folded map
we used as our coaster.

Until, Technicolor   Marlborogrand
beneath the goldenhoney smooth of a just rising sun
—America's Rockies—
not Colorado's or Wyoming's, but Yours and Mine,
and my breath…my breath…
"Michael, Oh, Michael" I cried
to the sleeping impostor beside me
who spilled the lukewarm last
of ice begged from the dining car
on his sock
and rubbed his morning moviestar eyes,
whispering low throaty   and true
    "So?"
then shrugged the weary of a son
whose father owns real estate in Aspen
giving finally, unforgivably, to exhaustion
aboard the speedtowest
of my first   hungry   train.

Learning to Be Good at the Jewish Home for the Elderly

Too old
I kneel next to this hard vinyl seat
and lay my head on the thigh
of the strange smelling old man

Mama's father   my Zeyde
His hand thuds
on my ear
then smooths my hair

Thuds on my ear then
smooths my hair over
my eye and across the nose that
everyone says is like his

Thuds my ear and gums Our Cookies—
We bought them—Archway!
Oatmeal *and* Molasses—until they are gone
He never shares

Mama knows   She knows
sees me kick away my patent leather
halts her Yiddish
       "Wait still, Baby.

     This
   is Good."
Then Zeyde   at last asleep
Mama lifts me to the lap of a long white stranger

—some other little girl's Zeyde—
a folded loose face suddenly alive as if Mama dropped in a dime
He bounces   and bobbles
his sharp bone knee   his strange language

spilling from his gaping slack
that I peer into
and down
as I hear

Mama say
        "Be patient,
        my baby.
        Be Good."

On an Asphalt Playground, 1972

What I saw
when I looked up at you
was your long
neck chafed pink
by Chicago's February,
so I reached beneath
your open collar and pulled
the coal black button
through the fake sheepskin lining
and matted stiff wool,
then patted my good work.

You looked from my face to
the piled old snow and kicked
       twice.
        "I have a mother," you said,
        and turned
        and turned to that girl who told lies about me,
        and did not return
           ever.

You liked to water-ski, I think.
Your father had a boat.
And my father always called you a long drink of water.
There was that night in pajamas
when we punctured our pimples
with a hot pin and scrubbed
first with Noxema,
then with lemon juice.
You already had a woman's hips.

That's all I remember.
I don't know if you went to my high school.

But when I dream of you
I make the steady pull beneath
for the stony button
growing slick and heavy
in my palm
a doorknob turned
                        turned
                                closed
                                            locked.

The Corner
for Rick

A mystery to me how they all fitted. Each cool, gleaming, tile
in our parents' hallway exactly belonged. One beside the next,
their jagged, craggy idiosyncrasies shaped precisely
to their brethren, as if formed of a piece, like the film
of ice that caps the puddle and crackles a warning before
breaking, and so, does not break. But just after Mom died,
two pieces came up under my rag as I polished them. I held
them, light and clicking, in my palm. Dad better not find out
about these; the glued down coming up was enough to cut him
open and who would mop the spill? I tried Elmer's.

When I scrubbed again the next week, they were already loose.
I took my bike and babysitting money and asked a hardware man
who gave me a tube full of promises, and, for a while, the floor
held. Remember how they would glow, reflecting a light mixed
of day filtered through the gold shears and the clear glass lancet
on the door? Remember their clay-round sound beneath the
dog's paws? On one side, the set-piece living room, on the other,
a closet stuffed with protection against winter. They led to
a stairway, which led to my own space, which had its own lock.
One day, I thought I heard the loose bits clink. A few days later,
the house spat its severed teeth at Dad's feet. I saw him bend.
He laid them in a drawer.
      "Your mom was after me to fix these."
Then he shut it. And there they remained.

It has come to me to write this today because I've been feeling
around you, looking for a way in, and over and over again, my
memory places me back in that corner. I can hear the silence
that fell, white, heavy, warm, when Dad and the New Wife
would finally just get out, sweeping their hiss with them.
Perhaps not silence, but the silence of a house: the refrigerator's
hum, maybe the snoozy growl of the heater, and then a moment
—something suspended—a moment that most of me almost
thought it could trust, when, as if straining though the gray
seams beneath me—your voice…how to describe that voice?
Like the earth moaning through gravel—that is, if the earth
were asthmatic—your voice, entering my corner.

I knew the unbroken smooth of your chest. I knew
your finger lightly running its length. I knew my choices:
on one side a door leading to a matrix of identical houses set
back from vacant walks, the TVs glowing, the upstairs lights;
on the other, a stairway, and halfway up, you.
    "How about a little back rub?"
Between the gap in the vestibule and a lock you had long since
proved would give way with just slight force, your voice circled
in the dust mote and settled.
    "Come on. Please."
No choice. No choice but to stand beneath my own brother for years
saying, no, no, I said no, so that today, there is nothing to tell, just
something that never happened, like a storm that gathers and hangs
but does not drop, merely freezing the morning dew into a shear
sheet, treacherous beneath a blanket, but melting in the sunlight.

Unwrapped

Because I wouldn't do it, call Stan "Schmucky"
like the rest of you, maybe that's why he dug me.
Maybe 'cause I was always there—Rick's baby sis, watching
Gilligan, mixing the meatloaf. So it just seemed right
that one night he and I would share a blanket, maybe
because I wouldn't do it, call Stan "Schmucky."

Who'd guess that from somewhere in the silence, you,
so studied cool, so deep throat, would say,
"Mind if I join?" Were you in your underwear?
Or just streaking the darkness? And what did you have
in your head we three would do exactly, blood brother?
Stan dogged me, saying, "Don't have a spaz."
So you see? There were witnesses
who'd guess that from somewhere in the silence, you

began the touching, the groaning, the please, the please;
who'd guess that every time we were left alone, you
began the touching, the groaning, the please, the please.

"Poor Rick,"
another friend said to me. "It must be so hard
to live with your sister when you think she's a fox.
Poor Rick."

        Your sit-on-it vibe, your in-your-face
        jibes, even when there was no choice
        but to be in the same room.
        Your sit-on-it vibe, your in-your-face,
        so studied cool, so deep throat,
        the witnesses blamed me.
        Mr. Cool-City, man. Mr. Party-Hardy,
        you could have let them like me,
        but you showed them how to show me
        your sit-on-it vibe, your in-your-face.

Come on. Cop to it.
In college when asked, you denied you had siblings.
I know. One of your Schmuckies testified.
You were freakin', weren't you? Freakin' I would talk
freakin' so bad that from somewhere in the silence you
sent a letter: "Families share a history," you wrote. "We do not."
Come on. Cop to it.

I never let you touch me,
that's why you were freakin', weren't you?
Freakin' I would tell. Oh,
how you wanted everything
and then you wanted more.
I never let you touch me

unwrapped.
Something so different
down there, so precious
that Mama oiled and
powdered. You wanted
unwrapped.

Poor Rick.
I came through the door,
poor Rick,

swaddled like a pink gift,
swaddled like a prize.

A Brief Thaw

I am estranged from my family. Or rather, my family are all estranged from one another. But recently I wrote my favorite brother with whom I haven't spoken in more than twenty years.

>   long shadows cross the lake
>   weeping willow
>   dips its bough

Weeks go by. It is clear he is not going to return my letter. I wonder if I will ever see him again.

>   too many leaves
>   where the river bends…
>   dry waterfall

A Poem for No One's Dog

My father's wife bought him,
wide-pawed   droopy-eared
for her sons' everyotherweekend
and legalholidays. She had to.
Their father already owned one.

So she brought home this pup,
unschooled and unstoppable
to leash me in
to train   feed   walk   brush and   have
a reason to go home each day.

She bought him
for my father to kick
whimpering and shocked across the basement,
to whip with his open hand
instead of her.

           Not like the last dog whom
           Mama called her last child,
           and stroked the long fur,
           the color she chose to wear her own,
           who faded and fell when she died, then
           died himself a few months later.

           Not   like   that   dog.

But like a dog who has a dog's life
born   beaten   forgotten.
A dog no one took photos of.
"I had him put down,"
my father's wife said.
"Wipe that look off your face.

It wasn't your dog."

No one's dog

No one's dog
—whose name was Max—
was half-shepherd
and half hairless with bruises
when his life ended in 1976
months after his birth.

No one's dog had
a pinkness in his ear
that spread before he let
me paint it with ointment
shuddering then sleeping
to my lullaby "i know,
little one, i know."

I guess he's dead now,

but in 1993, strolling behind him on Christopher Street, I'd thought he was a woman: his cinched 501s blossomed at the hip; his tiara of greased and groomed hair; his willow neck; his chin tipped towards a man whose fingers he'd laced, whose shoulders he bumped—until I saw the wound, purple-black as a beetle, five inches long, three wide, a seam of yellow puckering the surrounding skin.

"sarcoma"
that word from the paper
—fetid lake

My own arms, pink and solid, reach,   embrace a chill breeze.

In the Half-Light Before the JCC Single Parents' Event, 1978

The red and beige geometric leisure suit,
        I would imagine,
just the jacket, though,
        you know better,
and Old Spice, always.
        Kent Kings in your pocket,
rendering the Old Spice irrelevant.
        Keys to your eight-year old Ford
warming your hand.

You have to go.
        "Single?"
Not in your vocabulary.
        What will you do
when they ask?

        They will ask.

Focus on the fancy degree,
        the big vocabulary. Try
Jewish Bingo—5 people you both know—
        that one always works.
Don't tell them
        you have no clue

where your first boy is, or how
        you'll pay tuition
for the second. I'm all right
        to talk about,
laying out the eggs
        before you climb the stairs.

Don't say that. Say
        "University of Chicago."
What you need's
        a slogan: Widower:
Would Have Loved for Life.

        But she's five years
                dead already, so,
    no, that's not going to float, besides
            it's that next one
    that's gonna get you,
                pelting her hail from the North Shore
    to the South Side.
            And women, they want
    you to at least be checking the want ads.
            They can smell it.
        What with the jacket and the car…

What you need's a gambit, some door
        to get your foot in.
Hunched over the steering wheel,
        tapping your ashes,
you wait. Someone
        will hesitate.
That will be her. The one
        who is not sure
she wants to enter,
        who retreats
then rechecks her compact.
        This is the woman
to approach in the half-light:
        "Oh I hate these things."
"Yes, me too."
        "Why don't we just grab a bite?"

Talk about her.
        And quick,
lose the jacket.

Community Property

My father only marries women
who steal things from restaurants.

My mother, lawless for love,
feigned the slipped elbow,

caught the crystal ashtray
from the anniversary celebration

in her lap, because it had his initials,
then pocketed this secret shame.

His second wife,
dreading all things which too quickly pass

brought a suitcase to salad bars:
pineapples, full baskets of saltines,

grapes bunched like fists, hard pebbles of cheese
twisted in small napkins—

all good enough for tomorrow's lunch.
Now my father shares his table with a woman

who palms Sweet 'N 'Lows
into a pouch prepared for the purpose.

She bats her eyes, the innocent,
her hands coated in sparkling silver

thefts as thin as fine white dust
sweet now, but lingering on the tongue

bitter and changed.

The Stories of Survivors

You pack your clothes in the bag
put the bag in the trunk
drive to the airport
You buy a ticket for Miami
where you can lie on the beach
beside Jewish women in bikinis
and forget the two teen-aged sons
the daughter just twelve
who sleep alone in the house
you used to share with their mother

You want
the stories of survivors:
Auschwitz, Buchenwald, Dachau—
the company of those
carved out by misery
You like to stand in line
stamped   confirmed   close
Your bag seems to float
in your single palm
You will grow a beard
You will not be found

So many years later
you ask if there is still
anything left to forgive
and I say that these details
repeated for my punishment
have hollowed me
and I can float away
You say you have made me a survivor
Then you insist the odd cool key
into my open palm
Tell me the first paragraph names me, "executrix"

I ask, why the daughter
the last one   the lost one
and you say Mark
is too foolish   Rick, too greedy
and we laugh, you and I
for we have practiced laughing at the truth
Then I fold the key away
in one of my many pockets
knowing for the first time
I will survive you, father
and I have stories to tell

III

The Day I Suffered from Temporary Incapability

limbless
floating
detached
i search
inside
to find
nothing
but air
turn
keys
that open
emptiness
cannot
even
find
my tears
i am folded
filed
forgotten
behind
the ticking of the clock
stuck
in pockets
like fists
against the
freeze
in Pittsburgh
there is always something
falling
from the sky
alighting
like lace
upon my cheek
softening
to a streak
of sting

and tomorrow, green again

you are like this snow, lightly lipping my hair, then suddenly, blanketing a hushing gleam.

        all the world:
        this space
        between us

"i'm sorry," i say, backing away.

        blown
        in the whirling wind:
        first buds

you bow, already drifting.

        hugging the yellow line home
        even now
            melting

Is This Not the Nature of Obsession?

I pick up the receiver
    I return it to cradle
        pushing the buttons again
            —all day your face—

I return it to cradle
    Your face
        —all day your face—
            has marked the pages of my books

Your face
    pushing through customers
        has marked the pages of my books
            rushing towards me

pushing through customers
    from behind every thought
        rushing towards me
            impudent, laughing, demanding a kiss

from behind every thought
    Seven digits, and   panic
        Impudent, laughing, demanding a kiss
        Close the connection

seven digits, and   panic
    Stop the hand
        Close the connection
            Tonight I drown you with wine

Stop the hand
    spilling, wine upset, staining
        Tonight I drown you with wine
            across the clean sheet

spilling, wine upset, staining
    I have written
        across the clean sheet
            in letters as large as Band-Aids

I have written
    AVOID
        in letters as large as Band-Aids
            FIND FAULT

AVOID
    pushing the buttons again
        FIND FAULT
            I pick up the receiver

wave

parked beneath
the lighted tree
—shadows and winter

        beneath
        the lighted tree
        in love with the other man…

                throwing my penny
                into the fountain
                so many there already

        "i'm moving out,"
        i tell
        your ringing line

letting my car drive—
finding myself
home

Dear Rejection,

You are invited
tomorrow for tea.

Please bring a rhythm
to tap on your knee,

your ridiculous notions
your two-step and sigh,

a yarn to unravel, a riddle to try.
Please bring your whimsy,

your desire to roam,
but Rejection, please, leave

your reasons at home.

the sound of waves
on a moonless night
—distant friend

For Emily, On The Staten Island Ferry

we strike each other
as sand in the wind
words hurled this morning
slap us raw and open
in their churning wake
yes, all wounds need air to heal
but there is salt in this New York wind
this wind
that fills me
as i open my mouth to speak
this wind that filed you
sharp-edged and pointed
clouding you behind the fog and mist
that gathers on your shades

i remember when i did not need
my eyes to know your heart
before you swallowed The Apple
and saw me naked
all tear ducts and bitten nails
before you measured your world
by the heads you could look over
and leaned across the table, pointing
saying that i never knew you
that i am too hungry to fill
i made a cross of my chopsticks
and listened to the traffic
everyone going someplace
just to be someplace else

before we boarded this boat
to get a glimpse of Liberty
a woman whose height
needs bracing on the inside
who covers her metal with soft green
i saw her arms, muscled like a man's
twice in the mirror of your shades
before i saw us
there, lapping at her feet
two silver bubbles locked upon a wave
waiting for the next wind

The Night that Megan Called

Sometimes there is a sleep that cures
Sometimes a distance that desires
Sometimes nothing but drifts and canyons
Perhaps we should never have become friends
a Jewish kid from Chicago, a Catholic from Pittsburgh
dropped onto the sand bank between two beds
two desks, two cases of books, balancing
across our year of shift and slide
We closed land
You, breathing into silver
playing someone else's song
Me, sucking up smoke
spilling lines onto a page
We parlayed and approved
jestered and judged
lost focus and finally all sense
until time filled in the hollows with shadows
Still, you needn't have said your name
Your voice spanned years, bridged silence
to tell me the News about Michael
Oh, how quick are the living
to squander their connection on static
Nothing had changed
Men still tell you lovely lies
you still believe them   You still
try to get your mother to therapy
when she's not crazy, just Catholic
I still excuse my lack of apology
accept your judgment in crackles and hiss
No, there is no change
Only landscapes of drifts from earth
to sky, broken by gravestones

Blond and Strawberry-skinned

You stretch, supple and lanky in your black Speedo,
the dazzle off your ripples shoots from you like sparks.

Your words above the gentle break
of my sidestroke across the turquoise pool are filled
with boys and mother rebellion. You are nineteen.

This is how I think of you now.

Not waiting
        for your tubes to be changed,
        hoping the nurse can find a wide vein;
waiting to be rolled,
        examined,
        recorded;
waiting for dinner,
        breakfast;
        waiting
for the team
to open your young chest beneath close washing light
and fill you with
of all things
— balloons.

Balloons instead of lungs for you: a gift

because you know the name of your disease, scary and scarcely sounded.
Your mother found it in a book when she was trying to name herself
and now you are the book or will be after they test you,
    publish you,
        send you back to start again
with your gift of balloons.

Yellow, I hope,
full of glint
and the scent of chlorine
jasmine-sweetened.
Let them fill as wide as cloudless sky.
Let them carry and lift
across the tides,
and last as eternally as my memory
of your summer afternoon.

A Letter from Academe

Ann, do you remember why I came to Pittsburgh?
        If it comes to you
write it down. Use your skyblue paper. Use
        Sierra Club stamps.
I want to read it on the tiredbus, beneath
        the alwaysgray,
rub it when cloyed with Lebanese, hold a piece
        beneath my tongue
when marching in Harrisburg—marching again
        in Harrisburg. I want
to fold it like a glider that will carry me back:

        our last day,
the two of us, books piled between like steps into
        each other's minds,
smoothly-worn steps that led to a door I was shutting.
        I had to go.
I had to know. To know—something—to know
        differently. Not just
the surface I brightly skated sometimes stooping
        to bore a precise hole
but the pond itself, its depth and concoction.
        Any pond.
You shook your head. All a writer must know,
        you said,
is that she is a writer.

        Unconverted, I genuflected
            reflexive in the Knowledge Cathedral;
      divided my views like Gothic tracery, ever finer; pieced
           meanings from lofty colored shards.

Until yesterday, when that truck driver's story wound me
    over broken, unchosen roads,
and this morning, a seamstress wove all the right names
    for pockets and closures,
the way fabric shapes beneath assured hands and I found
    myself bowing again
before our steps, your blue-eyes reflecting back the me
    I left behind
just to leave here all that I have gathered. To gather here

    that the leaving is all.

Sure, perhaps it is this goblet, filled. Emptied. Filled again.
    But it's always like a watercolor here.
First washed gray and then the little colors laid on. Oh,
    perhaps it's hormones,
or twenties, or more rain tomorrow, but tonight you must
    call me clouds, Ann,
for I gather in excess. As I roll, fatbottomed, gray over Pittsburgh,
    I am perforated with pinnacles.

A Poem for Leaving Pittsburgh

This is an empty room.
Storms through my safe window bruise the scrubbed white floor.
This was me.
I sat in this chair and wrote my poems.

Storms through my safe window bruised the scrubbed white floor
between the Matisse and the Chagall;
I sat in this chair and wrote my poems.
Here. Where Sal stood when we shouted, "Surprise!"

Between the Matisse and the Chagall,
our plastic sled and tandem kite waited in the closet
behind where Sal stood when we shouted, "Surprise!"
Look, bus schedules I've never used,

though our plastic sled and tandem kite waited in the closet.
...Once my wind chimes would have rung, candid and random...
(Whole neighborhoods I never used?)
This is the smell of boxes in a dusty sun room.

...Once, my wind chimes would have rung, candid and random...
This circle is April when I leave at last.
This is the smell of boxes in a dusty sun room.
This is my view of the hills.

This circle is April when I leave at last
riding golden lights rising into silver sky.
This is my view of the hills.
This was Pittsburgh:

golden lights rising into silver sky.s
This was me.
This was Pittsburgh.
This is an empty room.

65

fade to white

I do not ask for details, I do not want to know, and besides, I think it is probably none of my business anyway. A boy. Ten. The son of a friend. Another boy, also ten, best friends, next-door-neighbors, sliding full of wind down, down, a snowy hill faster, gasping, now breathless—god, too breathless—now dead. One dead. Not my friend's son, the other—an asthmatic. Dead on a hillside in the blinding glow. What can you say? What does one say at such times? I see these boys in my mind, over-large, as if on a screen. I zoom my camera. I am told my friend's son watched his best friend die. I have known so many people who have died, but I have only watched death, the actual surrender, on film. Someone else's death. Someone else's loss. There is always a gasp, isn't there? A shudder as if taken by sleep? Was there a flutter of lids, lightly touched and teared by melting snowflakes? Was there an open mouth, starved for air, for mother, like a nestling unnested? In my movie the wind whips the snow vertical: a frenzied lace curtain, and we fade to white. The violins rise; I use my tissue. I wonder if my friend called this child his own, you know, only joking, like some people do to the children of other families that they are close to. My friend looks a wreck. I can't think of what to say. But I'll call anyway. I imagine my friend, lost in thought, lost, on that hill, wishing, goddammit, he'd been on that hill and the phone rings. He shudders awake. Damn that phone. Damn that phone. That's how he was told in the first place and now everyone is calling and needs to hear it. Everyone. Needs. Two boys on a gleaming hillside dragging their sleds to the top on a bright January afternoon. I think I'll write a letter instead. What can I say? He is not really such a very close friend, but I am fond of him and he writes sonnets so beautifully. I'll use my Japanese rice stationary. It is so pretty, to write a note on it is like giving a gift.

I always want to send just the paper. The jumble and scratch of my hand across its translucent yellow flowered field breaks my heart. How we ruin things with our empty ugly words. I wish I could just touch his hand. There, simple—said. I should just sign my name to the bottom of the pure page and send it. I write that his son is fortunate to have such a sensitive and wise father. I mean this, although it is none of my business. Another friend knew the boy too, taught him in the school for gifted children. A bright boy on a bright hill. But it is not him that whirls through my mind like snow drifting in a vortex, but the other, the living child, the witness, my friend's child. Did he hold his little best friend, so near to him, almost a brother? Was there a spray? Don't asthmatic children carry a spray? Did his friend cry for it? And as he struggled to help, did it fumble from his freezing, frightened hand, tumbling down, down, the smooth, shining hill? And then the numb decision—chase it? Or warm his windless friend?

Beg him to calm down. Beg him to breathe, just breathe, damn you. Or maybe there was no spray. Maybe the bright boy on the bright hill had cried, "Aw, Ma" and fled his warm home feeling big and ready and full of cold, wet air. How wonderful the world was. How speedy and shiny and slick. Oh, to be out of control. "Aw, Ma." This other friend, the one who teaches at the gifted school, told me a story. The child—the one who died—loved to write. He longed to be in a special group for special young writers. And he could have been, was in fact, for one year. But the next year his silly sloppy teacher missed the deadline and the boy was left out. My friend, the one who writes sonnets, tried to use his influence with my other friend, the one who teaches gifted children. But it was too late. Nothing could be done. The parents were outraged. My friend was outraged. But the child was philosophical. It had been his choice to trust the teacher, had it not? He could have submitted the application his nine-year-old self, isn't that so? My friend, the one who teaches at the school for the gifted, said the boy was applying again, this time himself. Dragging his sled alone to the top of the hill. Close up: two thin tracks carved from white quartz, pointing towards the open sky. Why does this obsess me? I am so protected. I never listen to the local news. All that ever reaches me, in the breezy breaks between segments of National Public Radio, is the very sick or very bloody or both. But this is real. This is my happy, funny, not-very-close friend's wrecked face. Am I a voyeur? I am so ashamed, but I cannot help myself. I am not used to hearing about two boys, both ten, sliding, sliding, sliding, sliding.

until...

In the back
of my closet,

        a black
        umbrella

                waiting

IV

When The Call Comes: Notes Towards Revision

I.1   WHERE WILL I BE WHEN THE CALL COMES?

in bed)
        turning over. Aw, I've had this dream before.

                                            "Hello, this is (510)...

in bed)
        Alarmed.   Alerted.   3 a.m.

                        ...Please leave a message after the tone."

- I will say
        "No."
- I will say
        "ah."
- I will
        have said all there is to say.
            —My mind will flood with so much to say that I am speechless.
            —My mind will flood with so much to say that I will not stop talking.

I will not dance.
There will be
no dance.

I.2   WHERE WILL I BE WHEN THE CALL COMES?

at my desk)
- lost in it,
        my words scribbled as fast as scratched.
- lost in it,
        my characters telling me what to say.
- lost in it,
        can't see
            –the screen though my tears
            –my desk for the drafts!

at my desk)
- pushing myself,
    the words pushing back.
- pushing myself.
    No   words.
- pushing myself,
    cntrl c, cntrl v, "Dear Editor,...your *publication*...I've enclosed:...Sincerely,"

I.3   WHERE WILL I BE WHEN THE CALL COMES?

standing next to phone, hoping it is Ken)
- calling
    from Vancouver (Austin) or Houston (Pittsburgh) or Edinburgh (Oxford) or Prague (Budapest) or Tokyo (Berlin) or Tamil Nadu (Latvia).
- calling
    from anywhere really: his destinations, my isolations.
- calling
    from the airport at last! Send out for dinner; catch a shower.

I.4   WHERE WILL I BE WHEN THE CALL COMES?

gone, gone)
- in the mouth of Caruthers Canyon, oasis of the Mojave, or drawing designs in her dunes,
    filling my eyes
        –with sunset
    filling my eyes
        –with moon.

gone, gone)
- The crackling kindling the only sound;

    a cell wouldn't have reception here even if I had one

gone, gone)
- snoozing into cushions,
    basemented, earplugged, huddled beneath heaped coats in that be-bop dive Ken digs;

    a cell couldn't be heard here even if I had one

- snoozing into cushions,
    30,000 over the Rockies,
    –full of my picks for the next Biennial and what I would do to improve that second act and there's still the BART yet, and then getting the dog ...
    30,000 over the Rockies
    –mid-book, Ken sleeping, and there's still snail mail and email before...

    (Has the monster gone?
    Gone, gone?)

Oh, they always thought
I made choices.
They colored me in
their sketchy outlines.
Then they erased.

This is not new.

I.5   WHERE WILL I BE WHEN THE CALL COMES?

I will be out)
- The fog
    will have taken away the trees and
        –I will stand alone within its walls.

- The fog
    will have taken away the trees and
        –Ken's arms will circle me.
I will be out)
- The sky will be clear and cloudless and scrubbed,
    and the hills, a new green. Pink fireweed blossoms
    shimmer the meadow like sun setting on low tide.
- The sky will be clear and cloudless and scrubbed.
    30 dogs, 20 people in the surf,
        –throwing a red ball for Jezzie.
    30 dogs, 20 people in the surf.
        –Jezzie, my old girl now, head in my lap,
        eyes lifted to the birds.
    30 dogs, 20 people in the surf.
        –throwing a red ball. Another dog.
            Put down her food...
                Sort the mail...

      "Please leave a message after the tone."

II.1   IT WILL BE

Rick)
- brusque bark
    I freeze.
    I tremble.
    I pick up.
    I don't pick up.

Rick)
- oddly gentle. Rick?
    I freeze.
    I tremble.
    I don't pick up.
    I stand, fixed.
    I reach, eager.

Rick)
- oddly gentle.

    (Has the monster gone? Who do I mean?)

II.2   IT WILL BE

Mark)
- phony Texan
    mining for a joke.

Mark)
- phony Texan,
    but shrunken, tired of putting it on.

II.3   IT WILL BE

a complete stranger)
- anurse
- adoctor
- alawyer
- yourcurrentwife

III.1   I WILL

1. go through my closet, pull out all the black stuff, check for missing buttons, fraying collars. Hope that something still fits.
2. get out my bag
3. call for a plane ticket
4. a hotel
5. tears…my tears?
6. dump all that black shit out and stand amongst it naked
7. stamp and kick inextricable tangles. You jumbled, useless, lump!
8. tears…my tears?

I will
not dance.
There will be no dance.

IV.1   WHEN THE CALL COMES

I will)
- know what to do/not know what to do/know what I know/know not to know/know to not will.

IV.2   WHEN THE CALL COMES

Ken will)
- want to come.
    > I will say no.
    > I will say yes.
    > I will say no.

Ken will)
- want to help.
    > I will say, how?

Ken will)
- be gone.
    > Karpacz, (Antalya,) Dagstuhl: his destinations, my isolations.
    > –I will
    >> send him email.
    >> leave a message with a clerk who doesn't speak English.

Ken will)
- want to hold me.
    > When the call comes
    > Ken
    > will hold me.

IV.3   WHEN THE CALL COMES

You will)
- still be here waiting for me like a chick, to regurgitate what I bring back, like your mother– like your mother.

You will)
- want something important from me
    - to shoulder some dark secret for you into the future, but I see you and won't give you the chance.
- want something important from me.
    - vengeance
    - one last slogan
- want something important from me
    - my permission
    - my forgiveness.
    - –You will
        - have it.
        - not have it.
        - already have it.
        - can never have it.

You will)
- have forgotten me already, think that I am Mom or your mom.

You will)
- want something important from me
- need me to finish something:
    - I will
        - –be what you need me to be.
    - I will
        - –not be not what I am.   This is not new.

IV.4   WHEN THE CALL COMES

you will be gone)
- I will look upon your face and see
    - nothing in it of the father of my youth.
- I will look upon your face and see
    - that your meanness ate and ate you until you died and that you never changed
- I will look upon your face and see
    - you all "Who me?" Blameless as ever.

you will be gone)
- I will watch you
    - lowered into a black hole beside my mother.

                    My mother whose will it was to be cremated.
                    Whose will you ignored.
you   will   be   gone)
  • I will watch you
                    falling from my hands like rubble into Lake Michigan –
                    all my idea.
YOU   WILL   BE   GONE)
  • I will
              hear your will
  • I will
              be part of it. You will want something
              important from me.
  • I will
                 not be part of it.
                    –This makes
                              no difference.
                    –This makes
                              me laugh.

IV.5   WHEN THE CALL COMES

  • …if it comes…

III.3   WHEN THE CALL COMES

  • It will sigh and shake its head and pack its bag and take to the dust of my attic.
  • When the call comes
              It will melt the stone in my yang wing and I will
                    let
                         it
                              drop.
  • When the call comes
              It will melt the stone in my yang wing and I   will   soar.
  • When the call comes
              It will clang the chambers of my bones in the wake of
              its pendulum.

- When the call comes
     The fog will wrap the shoulders of the Eucalyptus in its
     shawl and they will scree their echoing lament into the
     evening canyon and I will remember:
     –I will remember
          how you asked me to share your bed
          the night we buried Mama and how
          you held my hand all night long.
     –And I will remember
          how you begged me not to return to my
          own bed two nights later.
     –And how
          you wailed, pink and doubled at the
          foot of the stairs,
               "Why me"
                    as I held tight to the rail
               pink and doubled
                    as I left for school
               "Why me?"
                    until you gave yourself
                    a hernia
               pink and doubled
                    as I left for work
               "Why me?" as I left.
     –And I will remember the sound
          of your morning songs over your
          droning razor. What do you do
          with a drunken sailor?
     –And the sound
          of every door you slammed behind
          every person you threw out.
     –And the smear
          of the eggs you threw against the wall
          because they didn't come out round.
     –I will remember
          that you called me "Princess" and
          "Short Stuff."
     –And your hands

     as they released my sissybar
–And I will remember
    the dead smell of that rancid chicken as
    you pushed my face into it.
–And how,
    after Ken convinced me to tear years
    and years of your spiteful letters, they
    swirled like snow in a glass globe, silently
    settling, before I swept them away.
–And the flight. Oh, the flight!
    When you got your new Nova and said
    that I - little me - could choose the color!
–How you
    whirled me, crying out with the all
    the joy of possession "Red, yes red!
    Just like your tights!"
–How my
    legs sailed from you like kites, my entire
    being, my very life itself, trusted
      to just
        the grasp
          of our
            hands.

Conclusion

What thrives shallow-rooted, windborn?
The first fiddlehead of fern rising
from the tender scorched earth;
the clinging vine.

                              How I envy
                               the trees.

V

beginning

even before my own name
i learned

the fast folding
of fingers to fist

the flying away
again

peek-a-boo,
hide and seek—these

were practice, i now
see   even

before my own name
i learned   to say

good-bye

Dead or Alive: My Mothers Side, 1985

1-Zeyde

So you think, maybe,
it was easy?
It was not.
A man has got to know about things:

French dressing, they got here,
big bottles, small ones;
Subway trains! They don't know from donkey.

The kids got all kinds ideas of their own.
Who am I
to say no?
This   is America.

So, "Wear a tie when the boy from Rogers Park comes,"
she tells me.
And the next thing
she says, "Pa, go buy a suit for the wedding."

Excuse me, you wouldn't know I was here
if you could not smell my cigar.
and hear my fingers on your table
drum like Russian dancers.

2-Bubbe

What for I need English?
At market you speak with hands,
point, show the fingers for how many
how big a piece.
At home we speak Yiddish;
I say what I want.
And at *shul*
we speak
the language of the Lord.

3-Melvin

Stupidist thing I coulda done was sell that old car. She'd been a classic now. Those bugs run forever. I never took her anywhere anyhow, just to the bank every day, that's close by. Yep, had that job since I was a kid. Vacation, you know, I always flew. Went to Acapulco. Good time too, same hotel, same girl, 'course I married her a few years back, but we still go. Yep, I sure do miss that old bug, she'd been…

4-Rena

You have to say sometimes:
What can I do?
If your Ma was here
yeah, things   would   be   different.
She was a big one on family, your Ma.
You kids are all grown, you're God-knows-where.
Sometimes, change is nice.

Me, I like to re-do the bathroom.
I found this paper,
poodles taking bubble baths.
It's darling—pink and green…
you should see it with those fuzzy pink balls,
they hang over the window.
You can always re-do the bathroom, Bubbe.
Don't cost much.
Something new, you know?

You like this picture of us?
Me, I hate it.
Ben's nose looks like a sausage.
Ben's nose don't look like that.
I look so fat I don't believe.
You pay good money; you get a picture like that.

5-Ben

No one
cuts

anymore…
The job's

all gone…
Korea…

They don't wanna pay…

So now, I check
the bags at the Zayre.

…It's okay,
…real boring.

Time was when people knew each other. Sammy, Eddy, Jack and me we'd sit in the park and watch. The old men had a place under the trees. They'd share the paper. It was pretty good.

Sammy's still
on the south side.

Everyone else
went…I dunno.

6-Gayle

                Did I
              tell you
           my littlest
        looks like you?
    She has your eyes, your
    hair…remember the way
I would fix your hair? Like Cher from the TV.
     Sometimes Ma calls her
        by your name—
         my daughter,
          I mean.
           Yeah.
       She's the picture
    of you. Just the way
     I remember you.
     What did you say
      you look like?

7-Ma

Division Street does not connect
to Lake Shore Drive, even

via the University, even via
Rogers Park, even via

me. Eyes intent
on the penthouse

you missed the parade.
Hurrying, you forgot to finish.

Cousins, Unbraided

Snip the poem from the story: Eve Lites, Dippity-Do, Go-Go boots against the gleaming white tiles, *Teen Screen*, *Tiger Beat*, those elegant bottles that stood for inspection upon the mirror before your mirror—soldiers in a princess' court, or, bored, crystals to consult the future. Their suggestions: the back of the knee, the hip to breast—subtly shading, concealing, scented. All buried now, beneath a stone, a stone a log has long since fallen on taking half the hillside with it, its lipstick letters fuzzled, gray: "Rites."

(The homonym of that word, like, "I gotta right!")

Preserve the beginning: Friday nights, fanzines for guidance, you sculpting the Cher-do atop my willing neck. My ma and your ma kibitzing. Taster's Choice in your thin china cup, Pepsi in mine. My chin upon my pillow, all the way through Monday. The green chemical dreams. Snip.

(My weekly hair was the sensation of the fifth grade. Once Bobby Blaumiser said I looked like the Bride of Frankenstein and because I did, and because it rhymed with my last name, it stuck just as sure as with your green glue and pins. "Rites."

Then let the facts fall

away. Let your face unmasked, unmade as an interrupted dream the dawn that mama died, fall

away. You stood beside me as I threw my closet open. I let you choose the blue, (All right, one fact: Mama loved the yellow, loved it on me, loved it for itself) but I threw my closet open. Snip. Let my stubborn, liquid hair stream, so, stinging, I could not see that you would be gone in minutes, or maybe months really, but dawns don't matter, only snip – the sound of the poem – the falling,

the falling: a telephone cord, cut curled knotted tossed. Pick something up from Korvette's in Harvest Gold or Avocado Green, the clean new thing.

Gloss the extortion. The betrayals, treaties, surrenders, confessions, the economic freezes. Plots were played backstage of my brief and only scene. Enter thirteen. The steep raked stage swept clear, that phone cord, my only prop. (Though you did give me a box of threads, but that doesn't matter. In it, every possible hue. So what? It was thin and could be hidden; it closed with a soft "thup". I never used them but to touch, rolling the spools warm between my palms.) I say my only line:

"Without Dad
there is...

Act II: A silver party where my banished princess dances. But the King had his exiles – he was an exiling king – and Rapunzel, who had only hair to give, was as good as bound or shorn. From the catwalk drops a dime, glinting one wink before spinning to rest, then sinking. Offstage, the sound of a tree falling. The players speak some words which melt like wedding mints.

(And if surreal? Does the story end differently?)

All right. There was no princess—just a cousin; that's not much. And there was no tower. No, there were telephones, and U.S. Mail, and a school you could have dropped by undetected. And Rapunzel's prince, he someday came. It doesn't matter. Only the falling

Only that there was no happily, no ever after, just stones over which to stumble winding towards Woman, unsure at every fork, my hair snagged by brambles. I had schoolbooks to carry; I needed new shoes; and the woods are full of wolves.

The moon will rise with or without you. I will use her silver face as my mirror. She will not shatter. The moon will rise. I will stream my graying fuzzle towards her and sing my rites. With or without you the will will rise, and the moon will fall
             away.
With or without you all will
                    fall
                        away. Snip.

With This Book

Once, were I asked to weave my tale
I would have spun from lines of loss
a loose net, twice-torn, bound to fail,
and what was caught, no sooner tossed
from open palms to jagged roads
while mourning my own soil to send
roots deep. No place to reap, to grow
nor plant; no hay to safely spread
and warmly weave a dream called home.
But here I braid strong strands of lore,
ends firmly tucked and neatly sewn,
at rest upon my smooth-worn floor.
    Good-bye you stones; I'm off to fly.
    Good-bye you loss. Good-bye good-byes.

Wanting Land

Over the green hill
into the sunset
following you
I stood still for a moment
—as if that were possible—
and promised myself to remember
your body
that hill

And there
on that South Dakota slope
I felt my toes dig
        and reach
                and spread
I felt my heels
      find bedrock
I felt

    founded

Me   whose feet
only touched home
when locked into a lotus
floating and spinning
around myself

I wanted land

Land to build on
to soften on
to hold

Land with trees
to turn
and remind us
Where you would spread me
one final time

Our Land

We could scatter seeds if we wanted
leave our doors and windows open
dance on the bare floor
And winters
we would play our music
hang colored lights
read aloud

My feet
that craved Paris
Manhattan, Hong Kong, Nepal
now wanted only
to feel your feet
beside them beneath the blanket
as they carried me down the green hill
into your arms
home   home at last

À La Place De La Bastille, La Fête De La Musique

Tonight this latin-looking lover to sing to me
songs in French
songs in Spanish
this   springsteen-styling stud to lay the beat
just right for tonight I fête
I funnel unintentional through swell and bob
Though thoughtless
I may have caused this—
I have shoulders that long for wings—
they roll propelled by my song of just sounds
we make before language
find That Circle
where loose-limbed men loop one beneath the next
and sheeny summer shoulders do doubletime

Look, that Young Couple knows all the words
They act them out—the acrobats—
jig a jota   hoof a hornpipe
crash against the other like young and bored rams
Half His hair is magenta, careful braids and one
question mark slipping into his eye, the other
mouse-like, wheatstiff unmoving
He foots for Her a clumsy slide
She lifts one single line of brow over the unbridged aquiline
tips the brim on her greek fisherman
points with That Nose

to the band, to the sky, to the blonde venus
suddenly alongside tossing
glowing rings like light bells over hillsides
and I toss too and there is   well, a lot of hair
crisscrossing the summer solstice sky
as my hips, as independent
as adolescence, assert a widening arc

and I am caught here now and forever
in this circle of dancers
We are white, we
are brown, we are gold and winged
we are clumsy-footed young
men with men women alone babies on shoulders
we are hips   we are lungs   alive in this city of music
This breathing and beating city of music
Nous sommes des enfants   Tout est possible

Naked at 45

Like pampas grass, whose blush fades, whose reeds
desiccate and snap, or like the house left to weather,
sinking, soft edges fraying…there is no fresh metaphor
for my body, aging. An ordinary body.

A modern body, with its list of -ectomys
and -oscopys, -ograms and -plastys,
with its daily legion of iron-colored bullets
battling an inherited disease. A private body,
that leaves the boxes for abortion and recreational
drugs empty on the doctor's forms until they can prove
to me why it's their business. It has an ordinary history

of scars—one recently acquired! The most ghoulish,
something my mother never forgave herself for.
And in this day and age—and even though I've lived
most of my life as an artist—I have no tattoos
and only two piercings, one through each earlobe.
(I promised myself that every time one of my books
"made it" I would put in a stone, something permanent
and precious.) They've probably grown over by now.

My unkempt body: unshorn; unpainted; only cleaned,
polished, and snipped enough for basic maintenance
haphazardly tended to. A face that I am not ashamed of
and others seem to forget. (Frequently my dog gives me away.
Everyone remembers J.) A little disappointingly
short, and no one would say skinny. Carefully fed, though,

—mindfully. A plain body, in middle-age. Still, I remember
when Josie Burns told me I could fly and I did the highest,
farthest, *chassé* and *tour jeté* of my life, and I remember
running, effortlessly the fastest, the wind parting
before me, the other kids cheering me on, and sometimes
I want to. I just see a path and my feet want dash and I know

that I am not going anywhere. A normal body,
aging. This body that has filled its eyes with
the bright of clear sky over new snow, that has tried
through the night for the top of the volcano, that has
mounted the dunes in the moonlight, and found
its length in water and breathed, that has sung
the arias of love. This body that I forget to thank.

Vespers

Let me be willing to live my death
and celebrate its coming.
Let me say good-bye to myself.

Let my withering fascinate,
my whitening enamor.
Let me be willing to live my death.

Let me stop before the mirror and say,
"You were something then, kid. Yeah, you were fun."
Let me say good-bye to myself.

When it comes, let it come lightly.
Let it buzz and float and rest.
Let me be willing to live my death.

Let my breath, sweet music of my life,
fill and arc and fall.
Let me say good-bye to myself.

Please, no white room, no curtains drawn,
let me fill my eyes with evening sky.
Let me be willing to live my death.
Let me say good-bye to myself.